Mildred a...

SO-ARN-604

Beautiful
San Juan Islands
and
Puget Sound

Beautiful
San Juan Islands
and
Puget Sound

Concept and Design: Robert D. Shangle
Text: Brian Berger

First Printing November, 1979
Published by Beautiful America Publishing Company
P.O. Box 608, Beaverton, Oregon 97075
Robert D. Shangle, Publisher

ISBN 0-89802-080-8
ISBN 0-89802-081-6 (hard)

Copyright © 1979 by Beautiful America Publishing Company
Printed in the United States of America

Photo Credits

JOHN HILL—*page 17; page 24; page 32; page 33; page 34; page 35; page 39; page 40; page 41; pages 42-43; page 49; page 57; page 59; page 60; page 64.*

PAT O'HARA—*page 29; page 46.*

CECIL RILEY—*page 51; page 54.*

ROBERT SHANGLE—*page 38; page 44; page 58; page 63.*

STEVE TERRILL—*page 19; page 30; page 47.*

SAM AND BRUCE WHITE—*page 18; pages 20-21; page 22; page 23; page 25; pages 26-27; page 28; page 31; pages 36-37; page 45; page 48; page 50; pages 52-53; page 55; page 56; page 61; page 62.*

Contents

Introduction

Puget Sound country has been referred to as a ''sea which is within a forest.'' For those that have been privileged to navigate its many miles of cove-and-bay-indented shoreline, fringed by majestic forests sweeping to the foothills of distant ice-capped mountains, it is a description they will be comfortable with. Strengthening one's feeling of cruising above a submerged forest, many of the islands have a strong resemblance to mountain peaks. They are, in fact, just that. Ages ago the bay that is Puget Sound was a range of mountains that, through tilting and settling, and later by the gouging force of massive glaciers and the erosive action of mighty waters, became the sparkling inland sea that we know today.

Few recreational pleasures can equal the excitement and challenge of cruising the Sound's maze of tree-lined channels, which play host to thousands of eager boating enthusiasts and ardent fishermen each year. It is here, among hundreds of large and small islands, that one can still find the primitive beauty that so captivated its early explorers. Captain George Vancouver (discoverer of the islands) was moved to say of them: ''Nothing can be more striking than the beauty of these waters without a shoal or a rock . . . (they are) the finest in the world.'' It is a statement no one will quarrel with who has ever tried to obtain permanent moorage in the Sound. It was only recently that a leading sea publication stated quite frankly that the waiting lists at any of the ''. . . publicly-owned marinas (are) so long that your grandchildren may have the next chances of (getting in).''

There is no question that the waters of this popular resort area are the mecca of northwest boating—crowded to the point of having their own housing shortage. So many of its on-board residents have given up the soft comforts of spacious homes on the mainland to crowd themselves between floating neighbors. They adapt themselves to quarters that sometimes require them to live with just the very basics. They may know something the average land-bound ''nine-to-fiver'' only catches a glimpse of. A feeling perhaps of knowing the elements first hand, and having the personal satisfaction of controlling the movements of a finely-trimmed vessel is, in short, a breaking away from the routine, an experience of a unique form of freedom.

Besides its captivating qualities as a famed resort and pleasure-boating paradise, Puget Sound country is rich in sailing lore, and the intrigue of its smuggling days. The convoluted waterways that wind their way through the 172-island archipelago, those intricate marine "back alleys" of Kitsap and San Juan Counties, were appreciated early on by those that plied their trade in illegal imports, fine silks, opium and diamonds. In the roaring 20s, bootleggers found these same islands afforded protection from their pursuers, offering them refuge within almost inexhaustibly varied shorelines. Today, these islands are graced with tastefully appointed resorts and a number of marine parks, for those who wish to picnic near the shores.

In describing the San Juans, Bruce Calhoun (*Cruising the San Juan Islands*) has called them a "yachtsman's paradise," and tells of "the sheer joy of cruising, while viewing the grandeur of this wonderland with its gallery of magnificent pictures unfolding around every bend . . . ." And truly, the islands are a gallery, for like a real gallery the pictures are ever-changing. One views a panorama of seasonal shadings that in the mornings are further softened by a curtain of silvery mist; in the evenings, by the shadow-forming rays of a disappearing sun. Anchored in a cove he has just discovered, a resident of these waters experiences the thrill of earlier discoveries, and anticipates those that wait just beyond the next bend.

All is not sunshine in Puget Sound country; its weather, controlled by the air currents of the Pacific Ocean, is moisture-laden a great portion of the year. But it is *from* such a moist climate, says Robert Walkinshaw, author of *On Puget Sound*, that "this rugged land has taken for investure a wild and tender beauty . . . (picturing with) its ever-changing blues and greys, a far-offness, an untouchedness that is almost feminine."

It is this mixture of nature's changing moods that gives rise to the feeling of wonder in those that have cruised Puget Sound's waters or have driven her miles of scenic shoreline. To visit the Sound's Hood Canal area by car is to drive over miles of tree-lined highway that overlook that Canal's glistening waters, stopping occasionally to refresh oneself at some of its small townships. Or if one will stay for the night, he may wake to find a soft-white blanket of channel-nesting fog has moved in silently, waiting for the sun to lift its veil and reveal placid waters and distant forests. For those who would push further inland, the lush forests of the Olympic Peninsula await their exploring nature, with many trails leading through an emerald-canopied wilderness.

Puget Sound's beauty extends deeper than its island-dotted, forest-lined vistas; it reaches to the life under its waters as well. Here is a world of waving algae and sea grasses, where colorful giant anemones move their flower-like tentacles, where the crustaceans of its depths display their peculiar rigid dances, pulling back in crevices at your approach. Here, one can find the bashful octopus at the entrance of a rocky cavern, staring at you with disconcertingly intelligent eyes. Here are orange, blue, and pink-tinted starfish, their tube-endowed appendages moving them slowly across the sandy bottom. And here are its ever-inquisitive fish, eyeing your intrusion into their watery world, until they come to accept you as one of their own.

One has only to experience his first boating adventure in Puget Sound country to understand its wide appeal as a playground for those who love the water. Gifted with many moods, the Sound displays them in the greenness of its miles of curving shoreline, in the primal stillness of its sometimes fog-shrouded waters, and in the glistening summits of distant mountains. And always, there is the pungent scent of pine mixed with a faint, briny odor lifted from the water's surface by a gentle wind. Today, Puget Sound country closely matches the vision of George Vancouver, when nearly 200 years ago he wrote:

> "To describe the beauties of this region will . . . be a very greatful task
> to the pen of a skilled panegyrist. The serenity of the climate, the innumer-
> able pleasing landscapes, and the abundant fertility that unassisted nature
> puts forth, require only to be enriched by the industry of man with
> villages . . . to render it the most lovely county that can be imagined . . . ."

Brian Berger

8

Discovery and "Manifest Destiny"

That there is sometimes a fine line between imagination and reality, there can be little doubt. That imagination and reality are sometimes one and the same thing is the beginning of the story behind the discovery of Puget Sound.

It is the year 1592. Sailing a ship under the flag of Spain, Juan de Fuca (a Greek pilot) has been exploring the northwest coast of America, hoping to discover a Northwest Passage. Suddenly, on reaching an area between the 48th and 49th parallels, he spots a wide channel separating the continental landmass. Entering it, de Fuca explores its course for some 20 days; after which he writes: ". . . the land trended sometimes North West and North East and also East and South Eastward, and was (a) very much broader sea that was at said entrance . . . (passing) diverse islands in the sailing . . . ." Thinking he had discovered a passage to the North Sea, Juan de Fuca returned to Spain and the promise of a handsome reward. But many discounted the Greek pilot's claims, and when he died, he had neither the reward nor the recognition.

From his description, some believed de Fuca may have circumnavigated Vancouver Island. Others deem his story a fabrication: the dreams of an old man, prompted perhaps by fond remembrances of his beloved islands of Greece. Yet it is a fact that many of the land forms noted by this weaver of dreams coincide with existing ones. But 200 years passed before another explorer would make a comparable voyage through this "mythical strait," and chart it with capable accuracy.

That man was Captain George Vancouver, in command of *HMS Discovery*. Given orders to explore the northwest coast of America from the "35th degree of north latitude, northward to the 60th parallel," Vancouver set out with the *Discovery* and its consort the *Chatham* for a history-making voyage that began its most dramatic moments on April 29, 1792, at the entrance to the Juan de Fuca Strait.

Vancouver had by then given names to the landmarks he charted. Most prominent of these were the mountains Baker and Rainier: Baker being named for Joseph Baker (a third lieutenant of the *Discovery's* crew, and the first man to spot it) and Rainier, for Peter Rainier (a Captain, later to become an Admiral). And to commemorate the "exertions" of another crew member, Peter Puget, for his efforts in exploring the "south extremity" of this great inland sea, Vancouver named that portion of it "Puget's Sound."

The Sound's first white settlement was started in 1833 at Fort Nisqually (at its southernmost end), under command of the far-reaching Hudson's Bay Company. By 1849 the rush was on to settle the area in earnest: the mighty forests had suddenly become a prime commodity, and many small towns were quickly built around proliferating sawmills. Much of the lumber from these mills was destined for ports throughout the world, primarily for use in shipbuilding.

Because it entailed less expense to build ships where the wood was plentiful, shipyards came into their own in Puget Sound country and the ports did a lively business. Villages grew into cities, and places like Olympia, Seattle, and Tacoma looked to establish rail service with other parts of a rapidly expanding nation. Port Townsend saw its brief existence as the area's chief port overshadowed by the fast development of the Sound's other large cities; however, none of the intrigue of its Barbary Coast atmosphere was lost. Many of the timeworn cliches of the late-night seafaring movies were realities in this rollicking, promiscuous jungle of sea-weary sailors. A man could be shanghaied, or have his throat cut among the bawdy houses or the gin mills, where the law was at times as corrupt as the villains.

In 1859, the powers of Great Britain and America were focused on settling a boundary dispute in the San Juan Islands. Essentially it was the final showdown to resolve a loosely-worded treaty which in 1846 gave the United States possession of the Northwest Territory south of the 49th parallel, "to the middle of the channel which separates the continent from Vancouver's Island; thence southerly from the middle of said channel and Fuca's Strait to the Pacific Ocean." The problem was one of interpretation: which channel had the treaty makers meant the boundary line to run through? There were two possibilities: (a) the middle of Haro Strait, closest to Vancouver Island; or (b) the middle of Rosario Strait nearest the mainland. The choice would leave all of the San Juans in control of one or the other power. Both sides occupied the islands.

The Americans were particularly frustrated. They had fought a long verbal battle with the British for what they believed was their "Manifest Destiny"—the right to unrestricted westward expansion—that had won them the 1846 treaty, and were not about to give up the islands that they deemed rightfully theirs. The British, on the other hand, needed the islands to control the navigable waters they lay within, and thus were determined not to be intimidated by the Americans' push-em-back policy. Considering that neither the Americans nor the British recognized the others' claim to the San Juans, it was amazing that no shots had ever been fired in anger. But angry words had passed between them, and the time was ripe for a final confrontation. All it took was a pig.

It was June 15, 1859, when Lyman Cutler (living on the island of San Juan) saw a pig helping itself to his potato patch. Angered, Cutler shot the pig. The problem? It wasn't his pig! It was Charles Griffin's, and Griffin was British. Cutler offered to pay for the pig. Griffin asked for $100. Cutler laughed. Griffin sought legal means to collect, but Cutler claimed he was not subject to British law. The outcome of this seemingly minor dispute was the beginning of the "Pig War," which by August of the same year saw 461 Americans, backed by 14 cannons, staring down the barrels of 167 cannons mounted on five British warships, carrying 2,140 of the Queen's men.

Only the timely arrival of Rear Admiral Robert L. Byers, (Commander of the British Naval Forces) averted what may well have been a blood-letting affair. After being briefed on the situation, the disgusted Byers let it be known that he would "not involve two great nations in a war over a squabble about a pig." Two months later the arrival of Commanding General of the U.S. Army, Lieutenant General Winfield Scott, under orders from the Secretary of War, put an end to the whole fiasco by reprimanding Brigadier General William S. Harney (Commander of the Department of Oregon) "for allowing the situation to get out of hand." Negotiations extended over a 12-year period, ceasing altogether during the American Civil War. Meanwhile, the islands were jointly occupied until a final ruling in October of 1870, favoring the United States, finally ended the dispute.

During the San Juan negotiations, the population of Puget Sound country was growing swiftly. To move the products of this additional growth, steamboats were fast replacing the old sailing vessels, and there was stiff competition for the most desirable routes. By 1897, the wealth of the area was substantial, but none could have envisioned the economic windfall about to descend on them. "Gold! There's gold in

11

the Klondike,'' came the word. To assist in the increased traffic to the north, everything that could be floated was put into use. Many of these hastily-rigged contrivances never made it to the gold fields, their unseaworthiness ending in shipwrecks on the rugged coast. But many did make it, and it was not uncommon to find some ship unloading more than a ton of the yellow stuff before a gathering of amazed onlookers.

After the gold rush, Puget Sound country had a firm foundation of which to build the business of the 20th century. Economically stable, ideally located, the area continued to expand at a steady pace. Today, its riches are once again precipitating a rush. But it is a rush of a different kind: one that owes its lure not to the greed of man, but to the beauty of its natural setting.

Some Major Islands

The *San Juans*. The name has almost an exotic ring to it—it's really not a very "Northwest" name at all. It sounds like it would be more at home in a warmer latitude, conjuring up visions of virgin shores and peaceful coves, lonely beaches and waters of purest turquoise. But aside from the latitude, the vision is fairly close to reality.

The San Juans are an island paradise—but a *Northwest* paradise. This grouping of 172 islands is a tantalizing perplexity of "hidden bays and landlocked harbors." As one cruises the valleys of this submerged forest, the many islands seem at times to merge or change form, their close proximity playing tricks on the eye. Smooth, many-colored fields cut through the greenness of some of the heavily-wooded areas, their soft tints contrasting delicately against the darker green backgrounds of fir. Here and there, blue-belted kingfishers can be seen diving toward the water to scoop up some unsuspecting morsel. Ever-present seagulls, resentful of the kingfishers luck, circle the area voicing their disapproval. On the shores, other gulls can be seen perching and preening on rocky outcroppings; and occasionally, one will spot a seal reclining on these same rocks, looking like a well-tanned, plump vacationer enjoying the sun. Many small harbors present themselves, and one can see rows of neatly-kept beach houses, their occupants enjoying the water or resting close to their wooded backyards.

The largest island in this northwest archipelago is Orcas. Seen from the air, it presents a "saddle-bag" appearance. Its 57 square miles have nearly 70 miles of bay- and cove-indented shoreline. Famed for its Rosario Resort built by the onetime deckhand, onetime mayor of Seattle, Robert Moran, Orcas is a popular weekend retreat. Located on Cascade Bay in the East Sound, the main house sits on a foundation of solid bedrock, its contents secure behind foot-thick concrete walls that make up its lower two stories. The third story is of frame construction. To keep winter's wet fingers from reaching its imported teakwood and mahogany interior,

Moran overlaid its roof with thick copper sheeting—six tons worth! Never a wasteful man, he used heavy slabs of hand-rubbed marble left over after the construction of the battleship *U.S.S. Nebraska* (built in his own shipyard) to finish the massive fireplace that graces the dining room. Needing something to dress up this regal interior, Moran installed a huge Kimball organ costing $30,000, which issues its vibrating sounds through nearly 2,000 pipes. Finally, to allow for a colorful filtering of light to play about the walls and floors and to capture the nautical feel of the area, Moran imported a magnificent stained-glass window from Brussels, showing various sailing craft in the harbor at Antwerp.

Today, Moran's dream house serves as the main lodge for those wishing to stay and fully enjoy Orcas Island. Besides the lodge's generous quarters, a number of smaller units are available on the grounds to accommodate the overflow of guests during the busy season. Although the resort can handle up to 300 people at any one time, reservations are always advisable owing to its popularity.

Rosario may steal the thunder from some of the other, small resorts on Orcas, but one will find they too have inviting personalities. Along the island's north shore, one will find Bartel's Resort a pleasant place to tie up. The fishing is excellent in the area, and complete boating facilities are available. The island's ''Gold Coast'' are on the shores of its West Sound. Here, many of Orcas' wealthier families have built magnificent dwellings, nestled into the greenery of the surrounding forest. Deer Harbor, at the westernmost end of the island, is another favorite mooring spot; and the popular Deer Harbor Marina is an excellent place to refuel both boat and belly before continuing a leisurely inspection of this delightful island.

The second largest island of this grouping (and historically the most famous) is San Juan. Known as the site of the bloodless ''Pig War'' (bloodless except for the pig, that is) it is also associated with the romantic days of smuggling operations, its hidden coves acting as perfect drop points for contraband moving from Canada to the United States. The most popular moorage here is found at Friday Harbor.

No one knows for sure how Friday Harbor received its name. Some believe it was named for a sheepherder by the name of Joe Friday; others tell of the time a survey boat pulled near its shores and asked of someone walking its beach, ''What bay is this?''

Apparently thinking the question was, ''What day is this?'' he yelled back, ''It's Friday.''

But if you were to ask one of the weekend yachtsmen who frequent its well-appointed marinas, he might suggest humorously that it was named for the beginning of the weekend, because of the hundreds who head here during those magic three days. And one would tend to agree, for the sunny weekends do bring hundreds to San Juan's shores to enjoy its beach, and walk about its small town that is the county seat of the islands. Many good restaurants are to be found here, and after lunch, one will want to visit the shops that line its cozy streets.

Since 1903, the Marine Laboratories of the University of Washington have been situated at Friday Harbor. A finer location could hardly have been chosen, for the waters of the San Juans are rich in aquatic life, a veritable microcosm of the Pacific Ocean, but without the problems of its unruly nature. Here, advanced students in marine biology experience firsthand the wonders of underwater gardens inhabited by myriads of colorful creatures. The public is also invited to share in the excitement, with special times set aside during the summer months for their visiting pleasure. At the opposite end of the island from Friday Harbor is the luxurious Roche Harbor Hotel De Haro, a favorite stop for those who frequent San Juan. Its beautiful marina handles nearly 200 boats, and its airport is comfortably close.

Unlike the saddlebag appearance of Orcas, and the miniature "United States" outline of San Juan, the third-largest island, Lopez, has no familiar form with which to associate it. Quilted with a patchwork of many farmlands, Lopez at one time was known for its bountiful crop yields and dairy production. Today it is popular for Fisherman Bay, on its western shore. Almost completely concealed by a finger of land at its northern entrance, the bay is the home of the Islander Lopez Resort, famous for seafood specialties and Polynesian decor. There is protected moorage for about 50 boats, and seaplane accommodations are also available. Another popular restaurant is The Gallery, with free moorage available at its 165-foot dock, while guests select from seafood delights on the 25-page menu placed before them.

Shaw Island is the heart, or the hub, of this grouping of major islands. Though lacking in the large resorts found on the other large islands, it finds popularity with Indian Cove, at the island's southern end. Known also as South Beach, it is a long sandy stretch open to the small boater. A portion of it is a county park. Unlike many of the other San Juan beaches, which terminate abruptly in deep water, the bottom at South Beach slopes slowly for about 200 yards before reaching navigable depth. The island can be easily reached by ferry, which docks at the small village of Shaw at the northeastern entrance to Blind Bay. A visit to its museum, about two miles up the road from the landing, will help stretch the legs.

There are many lesser islands in the San Juans which deserve mention, but to fully do them justice, one would need to fill several volumes. Even then some of the smaller ones would be left out. By some estimates, visible points of land (at low tide) have been placed at 750. For a more detailed look at the islands, and some lore about the hazards of boating in these waters, Bruce Calhoun's *Cruising the San Juan Islands* should prove both useful and interesting.

Fort Casey Lighthouse, Whidbey Island

Sailboat on Elliott Bay
(Following pages) Sunset from Mt. Young, San Juan Island

Mt. Rainier from Penrose Point State Park

19

Camano Island State Park

Garrison Bay, San Juan Island
(Following pages) Deception Pass, between Whidbey and Fidalgo Islands

Sunset in San Juans

Seattle from Queen Anne Hill

Odlin Park, Lopez Island

29

San Juan County Park

Harbor at Rosario State Park

Tower at top of Mt. Constitution, Orcas Island

Seattle waterfront and Mt. Rainier
(Following pages) Deception Pass, Whidbey Island

Mukilteo Lighthouse

Rosario, Orcas Island

Totem pole, Washington State Capitol Grounds

Sunlit island passage
(Following pages) Rosario Bay at Orcas Island

41

Washington State Capitol Building, Olympia

Fort Worden State Park, Port Townsend

Evening, at anchor

45

Seattle from the Space Needle

Olympic Mountains and Puget Sound

Sunset from Mt. Young, San Juan Island

Port of Tacoma
(Following pages) Mt. Baker from Mt. Constitution, Orcas Island

Hurricane Ridge, Olympic National Park

Navy ships at Bremerton

Mayo Cove, Penrose Point State Park

Rainbow Bridge, La Conner

Tacoma Narrows Bridge

MARLYS

Port Angeles harbor

A memorial/amphitheater near Roche Harbor, San Juan Island

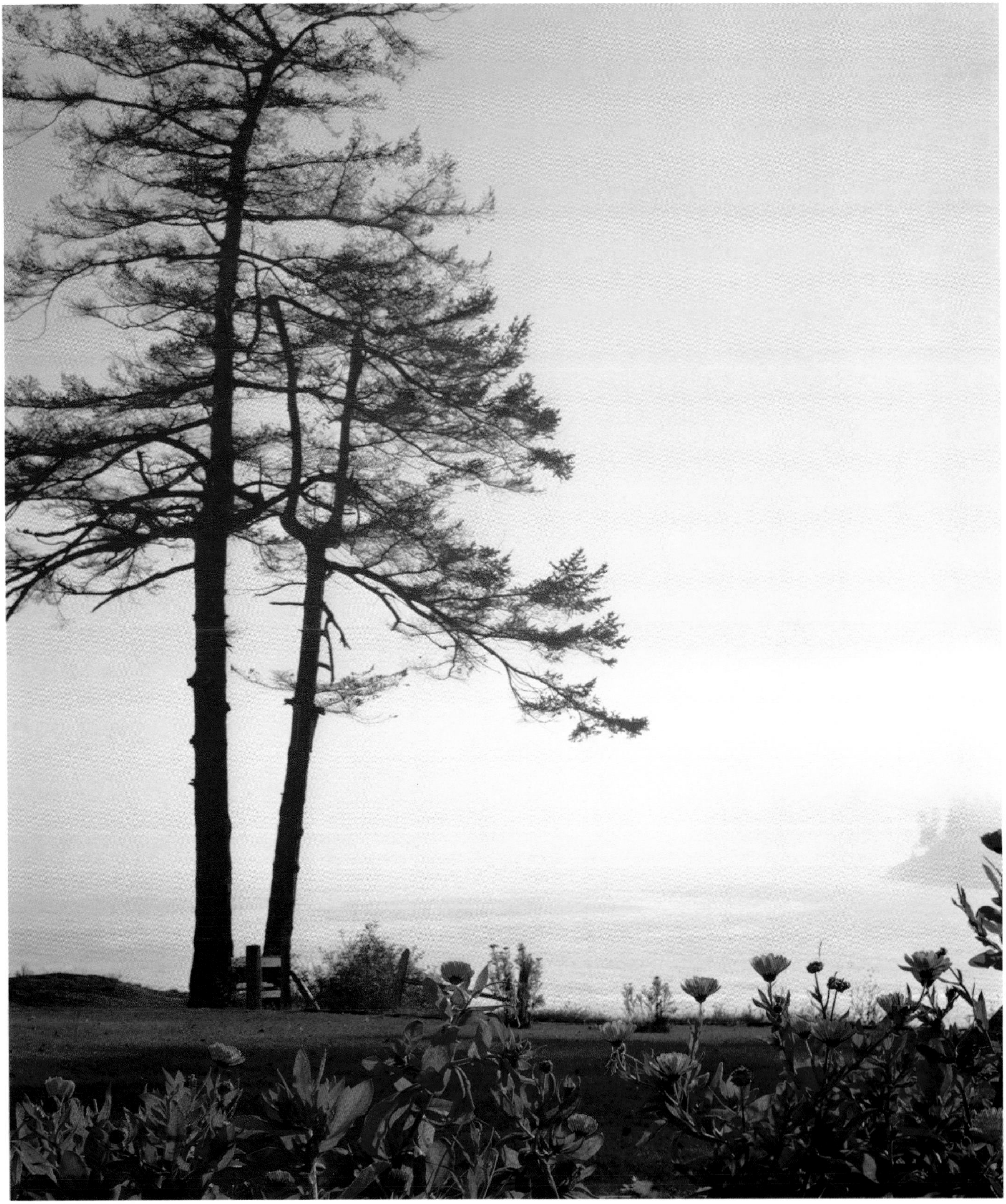

Doe Bay, Orcas Island

Roche Harbor
(Following pages) Rosario State Park

Boat docks, Orcas Island

Puget Sound

If one draws a line from Point Wilson at the northeasternmost tip of the Olympic Peninsula, thence to Snares Head of Fidalgo Island, he will have roughly marked the northern beginnings of Puget Sound proper. It is an involved network of channels, forming one of the most complex bays in the world. Measuring nearly 90 miles in length, its southern terminus is the city of Olympia. When he first named it, Vancouver had meant only the bay's southern half to be dubbed Puget's Sound, while the northern half was to be known as Admiralty Inlet. Time has erased any distinction between the two areas, and the whole is now popularly referred to as Puget Sound.

The largest island in these waters is the 55-mile-long strip known as Whidbey Island. Looking as if someone had gripped a long piece of playdough and squeezed it near the ends with both hands, Whidbey is divided into three distinct bulges. The island's largest town, Oak Harbor, is located at its northern bulge. Here, tourists will find many unusual little shops to browse in, some showing antiques, others the artwork of local residents. Not far from Oak Harbor, Whidbey's Naval Air Station is home for the servicemen that frequent the island's small towns during their liberty hours.

Coupeville, located in the middle bulge, also contains some interesting shops for the art buff. Its quiet streets, dressed with store fronts of another era, invite one to reflect on less hurried times. Not far from Coupeville, to the south, are the old gun implacements of Fort Casey. Built in the late 1890s, the fort was designed to afford protection for the Bremerton Navy Yard and some of the nearby cities.

For those seeking to camp overnight on Whidbey, South Whidbey State Park, near the northwestern entrance to Holmes Harbor, has numerous fine camp sites. Covering nearly 100 acres, the park has a beautiful view of Admiralty Inlet from the bluff trail skirting its picnic area. Boaters will find many areas of good moorage along Whidbey's interesting shores; and for motorists, the bridge at Deception Pass at the

Island's northern end, or the ferry from Mukilteo at the southern end, provide easy access to its varied topography.

Deception Pass, with its unpredictable tidal surges, lies between Whidbey and Fidalgo Islands. Fidalgo's major community, Anacortes, counts fishing and oil refining as part of its livelihood. There are several large marinas here, and after tying up, one can enjoy miles of attractive beaches, or visit the many curio shops in the area.

Just east of Whidbey, and connected to the mainland by bridge, stretches the Sound's second-largest island, Camano. Measuring 27 miles in length, it is covered in many spots by lush forests of firs and hemlocks. A state park with camping facilities is located near its North Beach, where trails wind through towering firs. The salt-freshened air of the bay mixes with their pungent odor.

Unless you know someone who owns property on Bainbridge Island, just off Seattle's waterfront, your excursions there will probably be limited to Fay Bainbridge State Park, at the island's northern end, or to shopping the arts and crafts shops in the town of Winslow, serviced by ferryboat from Seattle. Almost all the island's land is under private ownership.

Unlike the other large islands in the Sound, Vashon Island, just below Seattle's waterfront, has no bridge connecting it to the mainland. Instead, it is serviced by ferries docking at Tahlequah at its southern end, and Vashon Heights at its northern tip. Vashonites like it this way. They dread the idea of a ribbon of concrete cutting through their private preserve, acting as an endless conveyor-belt of cars from Seattle to the Olympic Peninsula. But outsiders are welcome, and will find the scenery—especially from Inspiration Point—well worth the trip. The produce of the area is a major draw in season, especially its currants.

The largest piece of land occupying Puget Sound's waters is Kitsap Peninsula. Connected by a thin isthmus to the Olympic Peninsula, it narrowly missed being an island. Acting as the eastern boundary of Hood Canal, it spreads its many bay-forming fingers into lower Puget Sound. Kitsap is the home of Bremerton Navy Yard, which sees thousands each year visit ''Mighty Mo'' (the battleship *Missouri*), on which the Japanese signed the unconditional surrender at the end of World War II. Largest of the peninsula's communities, the city of Bremerton is also known for its many fine seafood restaurants, which will fortify one for the hours of delightful browsing sure to be part of any excursion.

Another art-and-craft community is the town of Gig Harbor, just across the bay from Tacoma's Point Defiance Park. Easy to reach via the Tacoma Narrows Bridge

66

connecting the southeastern portion of the peninsula to the mainland, it also has a fine marina for those who care to visit it by water. For those more interested in the peninsula's scenic aspects, there are many waterside parks where one can carry a picnic basket, relaxing in the briny freshness of the winds playing about the bay. And for the motorcyclist looking for interesting vistas while enjoying the steady throb of his sturdy mount, the many scenic roads that cut through the peninsula's heartland provide miles of non-stop riding pleasure.

When one notes with what accuracy Captain Vancouver had charted the waters of Puget Sound, one finds it amazing that he somehow missed seeing the "great eastern arm" that doubles back for 12 miles after rounding the great southern bend of Hood's Channel. Of course, it was not Vancouver himself that had rowed "round the projection" obstructing his view of the cove's "whole circumference," but another of the crew. Still, as Archie Binns says in his book *Sea in the Forest*, one must conclude that on "his final look around, Mr. Johnson had forgotten his glasses; (or) perhaps he was tired of clams and did not want there to be any more of the inlet."

What Mr. Johnson perhaps was tired of eating, is today one of the big draws of the Hood Canal—clams and oysters. At low tide, hundreds assault its public beaches to dig for clams, or step gingerly through oyster beds to collect their lunch or evening meal. Highway 101 allows easy access to the fine parks of its western shoreline, and numerous small motels dot the length of its 75 miles of tree-lined highway. What is particularly nice about this stretch of shoreline is the lack of any large communities. Where the map says there is supposed to be a town, one will find a motel, a grocery, and a gas pump—with the only resident in sight the local dog, sunning himself on the grocer's doorstep.

To gain an intimate familiarity with the diverse shoreline of this inland sea would take years, perhaps a lifetime of cruising its waters. Yet there are modern-day explorers doing just that. Their love for its many islands seems to grow with every mile sailed, every cove explored. Here, one is gently rocked to the music of its waters, awed by the brilliant sweep of a sunset-painted sky, free of the concrete ribbons that tell one where to turn, where to stop. Here one is in touch with solitude, and given to the same forces that stirred its first explorers.

Mainland Ports-of-Call

Most of Washington State's major cities are located along the shores of Puget Sound. They, and the whole of Puget Sound country, comprise the heart of this great state. Its economic pulse feeds through the arteries of major highways, and flows through the channels of its inland sea. A visit to any of these thriving ports, either by land, air, or water, uncovers another interesting dimension to an already fascinating region of winding waterways and history-rich islands.

Much time could be spent extolling the pleasures that await in the Sound's better-known ports-of-call; Seattle, Tacoma, Everett, etc., but an abundance of information is readily available on these. Instead, let us drift into some of the less publicized anchorages, and perhaps discover the flavor of an earlier era.

One would never guess that Port Townsend (located on the northeast tip of the Olympic Peninsula) was ever more than the quiet, art-oriented community that visitors are familiar with today. Yet in 1890, this community of 5,000 was a bustling, brawling city of 20,000. Port Townsend had dreams of becoming the region's "Key City," and its population had grown in the wake of rumors that it would soon be serviced by a transcontinental railroad. The dream never materialized. Seattle stole Port Townsend's thunder with more expensive port facilities, and the railroad that Port Townsend had set its hopes on went to Seattle instead.

To visit Port Townsend's main thoroughfare is to step back in time. Its early brick structures, with their restored facades, house many intriguing art and antique shops. Strolling through any of its neighborhoods, one will see beautiful examples of Victorian craftsmanship, in the stately homes lining its streets. During the month of October, the annual "Wooden Boat Festival" will reward those who appreciate the nearly-lost art of wooden boat building with magnificent examples of contemporary and vintage productions of master craftsmen. And for those wishing to enjoy the greenery of the town's outskirts, a number of state parks have sprung up around the sites of old forts, offering acres of quiet woods, and access to clam-rich beaches.

La Conner, separated by Skagit Bay from the northern end of Whidbey Island, is another Puget Sound community that turns back the clock. This small fishing village of 650 people, with its colorful wharves and picturesque Mt. Baker as a backdrop, is home for many talented artists and writers. Smoked fish can be had at the Swinomish Indian Fish Co. nearby, while for those that prefer eating out, a number of nostalgically-decorated cafes offer tasty fare. To see where much of Washington's history was printed when it was first news, walk down First Street to the offices of the *Puget Sound Mail.* Started in 1873, the paper is still in operation, and prides itself on printing with the very press that issued its first paper.

The Port of Edmonds, between Everett and Seattle, is a convenient stopover for boaters heading north or south via the Saratoga Passage. Its small harbor is protected by a rock breakwater and is well marked in all areas. Built in the 1880s, the city of Edmonds took its livelihood from the surrounding forests, by converting them into shingles. During its most productive period, 10 mills were in operation, and steamboats called for cargoes at "Brackett's Landing"—named for the man that built it, George Brackett. Visitors here will find many fine restaurants, to curb an appetite made all the more ravenous by the freshness of the harbor's air. Curio shops are plentiful, and a delightful afternoon can be spent strolling the town's friendly streets.

Not far south of the city of Tacoma lies the town of Steilacoom. As in many of the small towns that dot Puget Sound's shoreline, the structures of an earlier day have been tastefully restored, and its residents go about the business heedless of the frantic building efforts of the larger cities. Though only housing a population of about 3,000, Steilacoom has its own history, as well as that of the surrounding area, well preserved in its Steilacoom Historical Society Museum, located in the basement of the town hall. Always a pleasant place to stop, perhaps just to enjoy romping about its Sunnyside Beach, it is especially pleasant when in July, its annual Salmon Bake is held on the beach. Cooked Indian-fashion around a bed of glowing coals, the salmon split open and held upright by surrounding stakes, the aroma carries to every famished bystander. Old tales are told, and ritual dances performed, and one is again reminded that long before the white man named these waters Puget Sound, the Indians fished and hunted here, and called them by the name Whulge.

To visit the town of Shelton by water is to negotiate a fjord-like maze of branching channels at the southern terminus of Puget Sound. Located on the westernmost finger of this watery hand, where forests form a lush, green backdrop, one is reminded of the town's early logging origins, which today are still a viable part of its economy. Simpson Timber Company is its main employer, using updated methods of timber management and maximizing the usage of every log they process. The plant stands as an example of intelligent forestry use.

South of town is the Olympia Oyster Company, where during weekdays a plant visitor can purchase mouthwatering specimens of Pacific and Olympia oysters, or Manila clams. In town, one can savor these same delicacies served steaming at a number of the town's fine restaurants, and then visit the gift shops that specialize in crafts of the local area. In May, the local loggers exhibit their sawing and chopping skills during the town's annual four-day Mason County Forest Festival, topped off by a Paul Bunyan parade that has everyone participating in the festivities.

From Shelton, a short drive across the lower end of Kitsap Peninsula via Highway 101 will bring a motorist to the town of Hoodsport, near the southern end of Hood Canal. Lunch or dinner can be had at the Hoodsport Cafe, Skipper John's, or the Old Mill, and one will find their offerings of goeduck or shrimpburger a top taste treat. There is a state fish hatchery nearby that welcomes visitors, or one can drive another four miles inland to Lake Cushman for a view of its sparkling waters, and perhaps spend a night at Lake Cushman Resort.

There are many such small towns dotting the shores of Puget Sound country, where one can always expect a neighborly reception, and a view of a lifestyle far removed from the breakneck pace of Big City folk. Many backroads lead to quiet lakes and towering forests of primitive stillness, where moss-covered bending spruce form cathedral-like arches over the soft emerald ''rug'' of the forest floor.

Populous as some areas of the Sound are, there is still a wildness here that touches on the primal state. Quiet stretches of sandy beach invite inspection, distant mountains urge one to find their foothills. Its climate lies moody at times upon the soft-colored vistas. At sunset, its western horizon is sometimes bathed with liquid reds and burning golds, seen melting quickly into its forests of blue fir. When the sun has finally set, and dusk moves quietly across the land, the waters of the Sound take on the deepening purple glow of approaching night. Near the shoreline, the silent soarings of roost-seeking gulls disappear against the grey of shadowed cliffs. The forest animals lie still, snuggling into the deep moss of its flooring. At times, the pale-ivory glow of a full moon paints the waters with liquid silver and rains upon the forests an eerie radiance. And always, there is the stillness, at times seeming unnatural, accustomed as we are to the constant din of our work-a-day worlds, but one that encourages introspection and a deepening appreciation of the beauty that is Puget Sound country.

Enlarged Prints

Most of the photography in this book is available as photographic
enlargements. Send self-addressed, stamped envelope for information.
For a complete product catalog, send $1.00.
Beautiful America Publishing Company
P.O. Box 608
Beaverton, Oregon 97075

Beautiful America Publishing Company

The nation's foremost publisher of quality color photography

Current Books

Alaska, Arizona, British Columbia, California, California Vol. II, California Coast, California Desert, California Missions, Colorado, Florida, Georgia, Hawaii, Idaho, Illinois, Los Angeles, Maryland, Michigan, Michigan Vol. II, Minnesota, Montana, Montana Vol. II, Mt. Hood (Oregon), New Mexico, New York, Northern California, Northern California Vol. II, North Idaho, Oregon, Oregon Vol. II, Oregon Coast, Oregon Country, Pennsylvania, Portland, San Diego, San Francisco, San Juan Islands, Seattle, Texas, Utah, Virginia, Washington, Washington Vol. II, Washington D.C., Wisconsin, Yosemite National Park

Forthcoming Books

California Mountains, Indiana, Kentucky, Las Vegas, Massachusetts, Mississippi, Missouri, Nevada, New Jersey, North Carolina, Oklahoma, Ozarks, Rocky Mountains, South Carolina, Tennessee, Vermont, Wyoming

Large Format, Hardbound Books

Beautiful America, Beauty of California, Glory of Nature's Form, Lewis & Clark Country, Western Impressions